STEAM JOB? DREAM JOB!

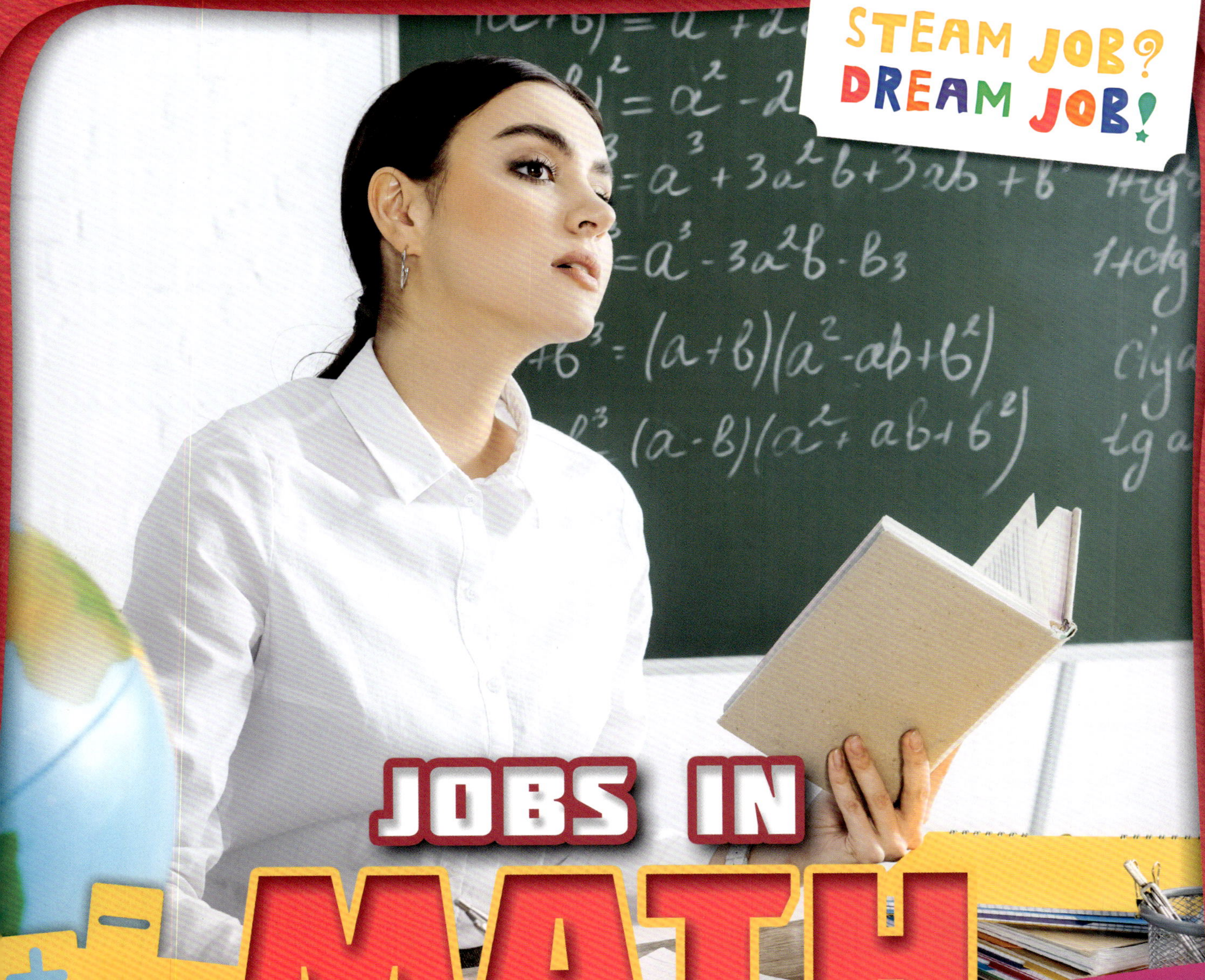

JOBS IN MATH

By Bethany Latham

KidHaven PUBLISHING

I0807168

Published in 2026 by
KidHaven Publishing, an Imprint of
Greenhaven Publishing, LLC
2544 Clinton St., Buffalo, NY 14224

© 2025 BookLife Publishing Ltd.

Written by: Bethany Latham
Edited by: Rebecca Phillips-Bartlett
Designed by: Rob Delph

All facts, statistics, web addresses, and URLs in this book were verified as valid and accurate at time of writing. No responsibility for any changes to external websites or references can be accepted by either the author or publisher.

Cataloging-in-Publication Data

Names: Latham, Bethany.
Title: Jobs in math / Bethany Latham.
Description: Buffalo, NY : KidHaven Publishing, 2026. | Series: STEAM job? Dream job! | Includes glossary and index.
Identifiers: ISBN 9781534552180 (pbk.) | ISBN 9781534552197 (library bound) | ISBN 9781534552203 (ebook)
Subjects: LCSH: Mathematics--Vocational guidance--Juvenile literature.
Classification: LCC QA10.5 L384 2026 | DDC 510.23--dc23

All rights reserved.
No part of this book may be reproduced in any form without permission in writing from the publisher, except by a reviewer.

Printed in China

CPSIA compliance information: Batch #QW26KH: For further information contact Greenhaven Publishing LLC at 1-844-317-7404.

Please visit our website, www.greenhavenpublishing.com. For a free color catalog of all our high-quality books, call toll free 1-844-317-7404 or fax 1-844-317-7405.

Find us on

IMAGE CREDITS

Images courtesy of Shutterstock.com, unless otherwise stated.

Cover – LightField Studios, Vadim Almiev, YamabikaY, Mechanic Design, James Kopina. 2–3 – Gorodenkoff, Anuchit kamsongmueang, urfin, Mechanic Design, James Kopina. 4–5 – PeopleImages.com – Yuri A, Gorodenkoff, 1st footage, Svitlana Hulko, Stock 4you, Nsit. 6–7 – Kamil Zajaczkowski, Gorodenkoff, Mechanic Design, James Kopina. 8–9 – Gorodenkoff, PeopleImages.com – Yuri A, Alexzel. 10–11 – Andrey_Popov, David Gyung, Dilen. 12–13 – Gorodenkoff, Cast Of Thousands, Fireofheart. 14–15 – WUT.ANUNAI, Lee Charlie, urfin. 16–17 – Anuchit kamsongmueang, Monkey Business Images. 18–19 – DC Studio, Nsit. 20–21 – PitukTV, Fineart1. 22–23 – voronaman, goodluz, PIMNADA, riabchevskii. 24 – Nsit, Fireofheart. Vectors used throughout – Vadim Almiev, YamabikaY.

CONTENTS

Words that look like **this** can be found in the glossary on page 24.

ALL ABOUT STEAM

Do you know what you want to do when you grow up? You could have a **career** in STEAM. STEAM careers use science, technology, engineering, the arts, and math.

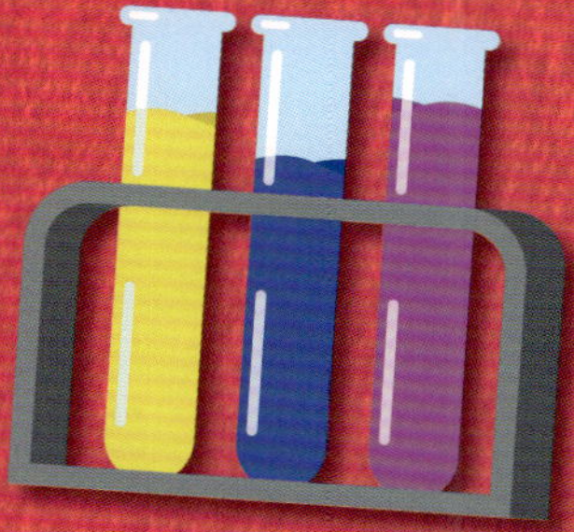

There are many different STEAM careers. You could work with animals, create video games, or even **predict** the weather. The skills you learn in STEAM classes at school can help you do amazing jobs.

ALL ABOUT MATH

Math is the study of numbers, shapes, and patterns. It is used in many ways. Pure mathematics involves studying math simply to learn more about it. Applied mathematics uses math to solve real-world problems.

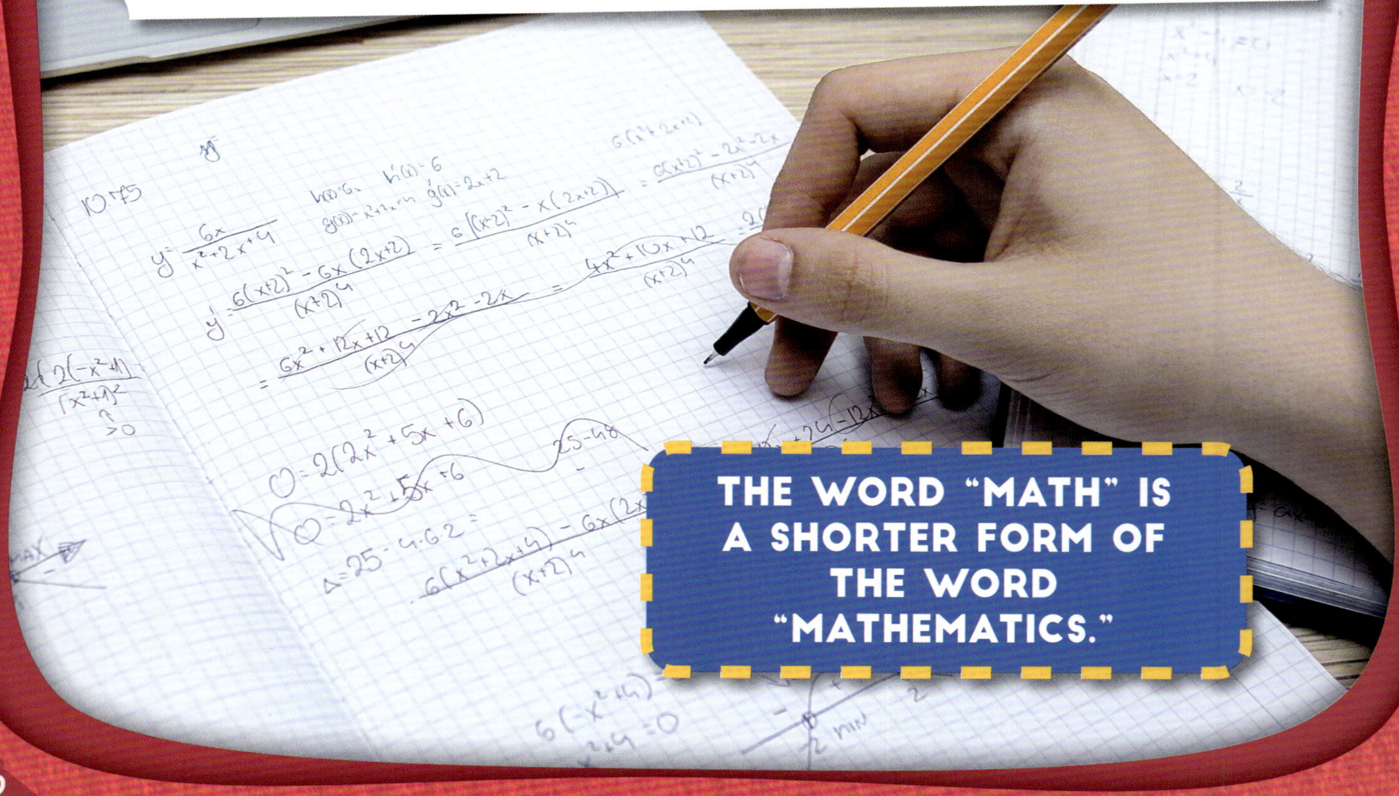

THE WORD "MATH" IS A SHORTER FORM OF THE WORD "MATHEMATICS."

Many things could not exist or work without math. Many jobs use math in many different ways. Math might be used to collect information, plan buildings, or develop our understanding of the world.

URBAN PLANNER

Urban planners design towns and cities. They decide how space will be used and how cities will grow. Urban planners create plans to give cities what they need, such as enough buses and trains.

URBAN PLANNERS ARE ALSO CALLED TOWN OR CITY PLANNERS.

Good math skills are very helpful for urban planners. They look at lots of information, or data. They must figure out how much their plans will cost and how everything will fit together.

AUDITOR

Auditors usually work for businesses. They look at records showing how much money the business has spent. Auditors make sure everything adds up properly. They also report mistakes they find in those records.

SOME AUDITORS LOOK AT WHETHER BUSINESSES ARE FOLLOWING RULES PROPERLY.

Auditors gather information, create **spreadsheets**, and make sure everything is correct. Auditors need very good math skills. They must be confident with numbers and good with data. They also need lots of patience.

STATISTICIAN

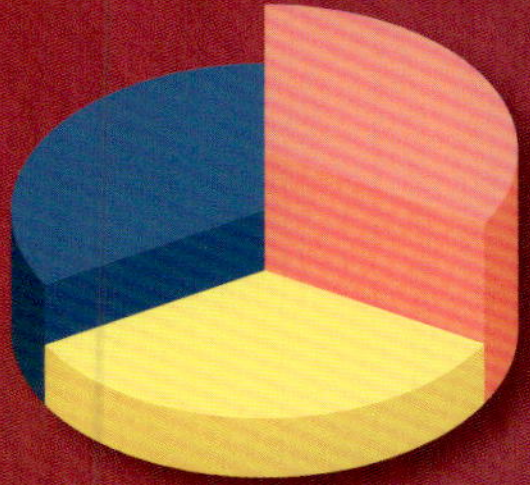

Statisticians collect data about the world and look for patterns to figure out what it means. Statisticians collect information about many things, including sports, jobs, and people's health. The information is often used for research.

STATISTICIANS OFTEN MAKE CHARTS AND GRAPHS USING THE INFORMATION THEY COLLECT.

Statisticians get information from news sources and reports. They also carry out experiments and **surveys**. Statisticians might give **governments** advice about new laws. Statisticians need to be good at spotting patterns.

ARCHITECT

Architects plan, design, and help build buildings. They might also help fix old buildings. Architects might design one building at a time or work on many at once, such as groups of houses.

ARCHITECTS MAKE PLANS CALLED BLUEPRINTS. THEY USED TO BE DRAWN ON BLUE PAPER.

Architects need to make sure the buildings they design are safe. Architects need very good math skills. They need a good understanding of **geometry** and good planning skills. Architects train for many years.

MATHEMATICIAN

Mathematicians study math to understand it better. They use math to solve problems and prove **theorems**. They do lots of research. Many mathematicians work at universities.

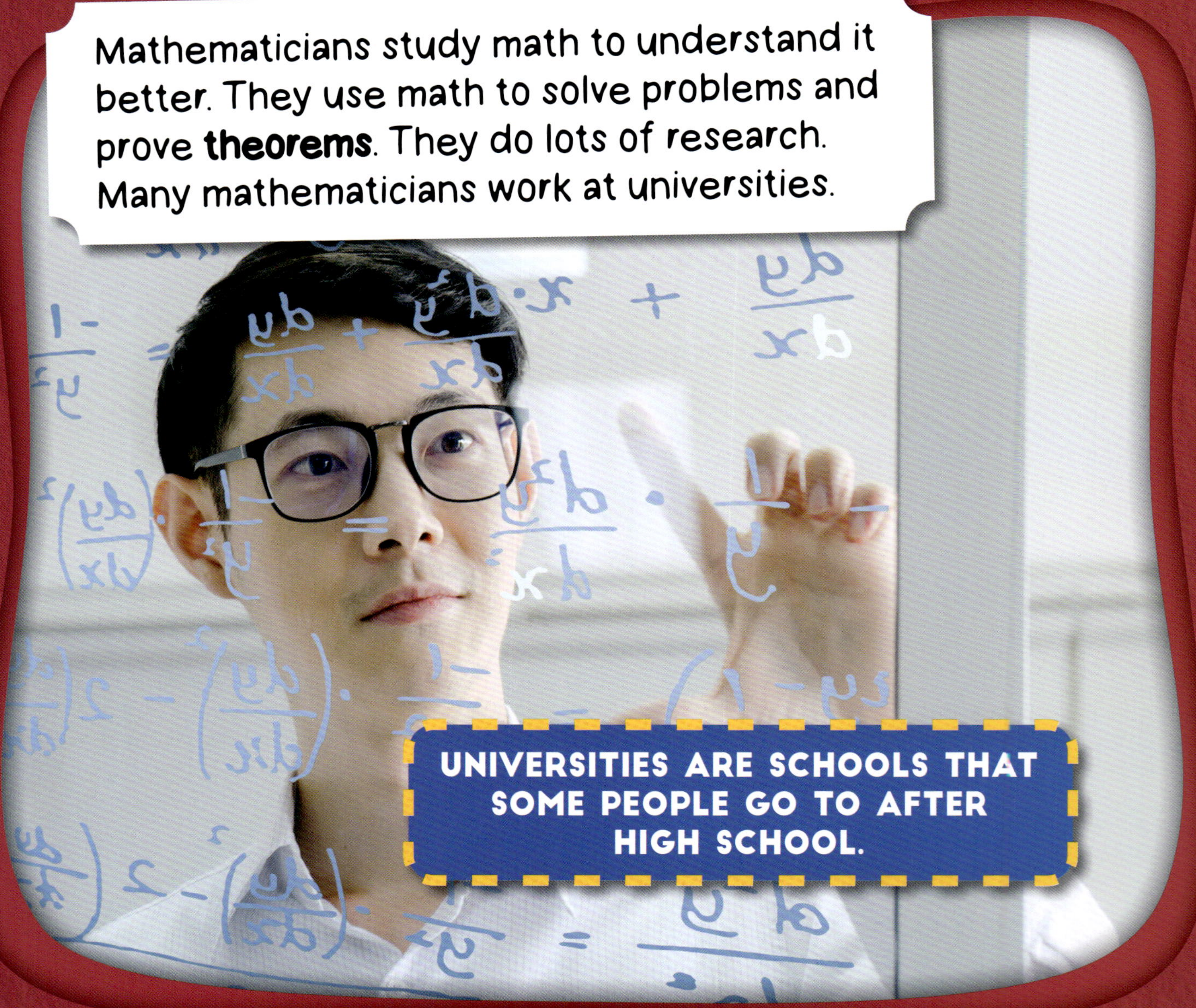

UNIVERSITIES ARE SCHOOLS THAT SOME PEOPLE GO TO AFTER HIGH SCHOOL.

Many mathematicians are **specialists** in one type of math, such as geometry. They become experts in their chosen subject. Some mathematicians might teach what they are studying to students.

BE INSPIRED!

ASK QUESTIONS IN YOUR MATH CLASSES.

VIDEO GAME DEVELOPER

Video game developers work as part of teams that make video games. Designers plan the game, then developers write the **code** that makes the game work. Video game developers usually work in studios with other people.

BE INSPIRED!

ASK QUESTIONS ABOUT HOW VIDEO GAMES ARE MADE.

Developers sometimes focus on one kind of game. They do lots of tests to make sure the game is working properly. Video game developers use math and technology skills.

METEOROLOGIST

Meteorologists study the weather and predict what it might do. Meteorologists study **temperature**, wind speeds, how humid the air is, and more. Meteorologists predict when big weather events, such as storms, will happen.

WEATHER FORECASTS ARE REPORTS ABOUT WHAT THE WEATHER MIGHT DO.

Many meteorologists share their forecasts on television, the internet, and the radio. Meteorologists need good math and science skills to make their predictions as accurate, or correct, as possible.

THE POWER OF STEAM

We have looked at some exciting math jobs. There are many more you can discover! Math helps us understand the world better and allows us to do many things. Many jobs use math knowledge and skills.

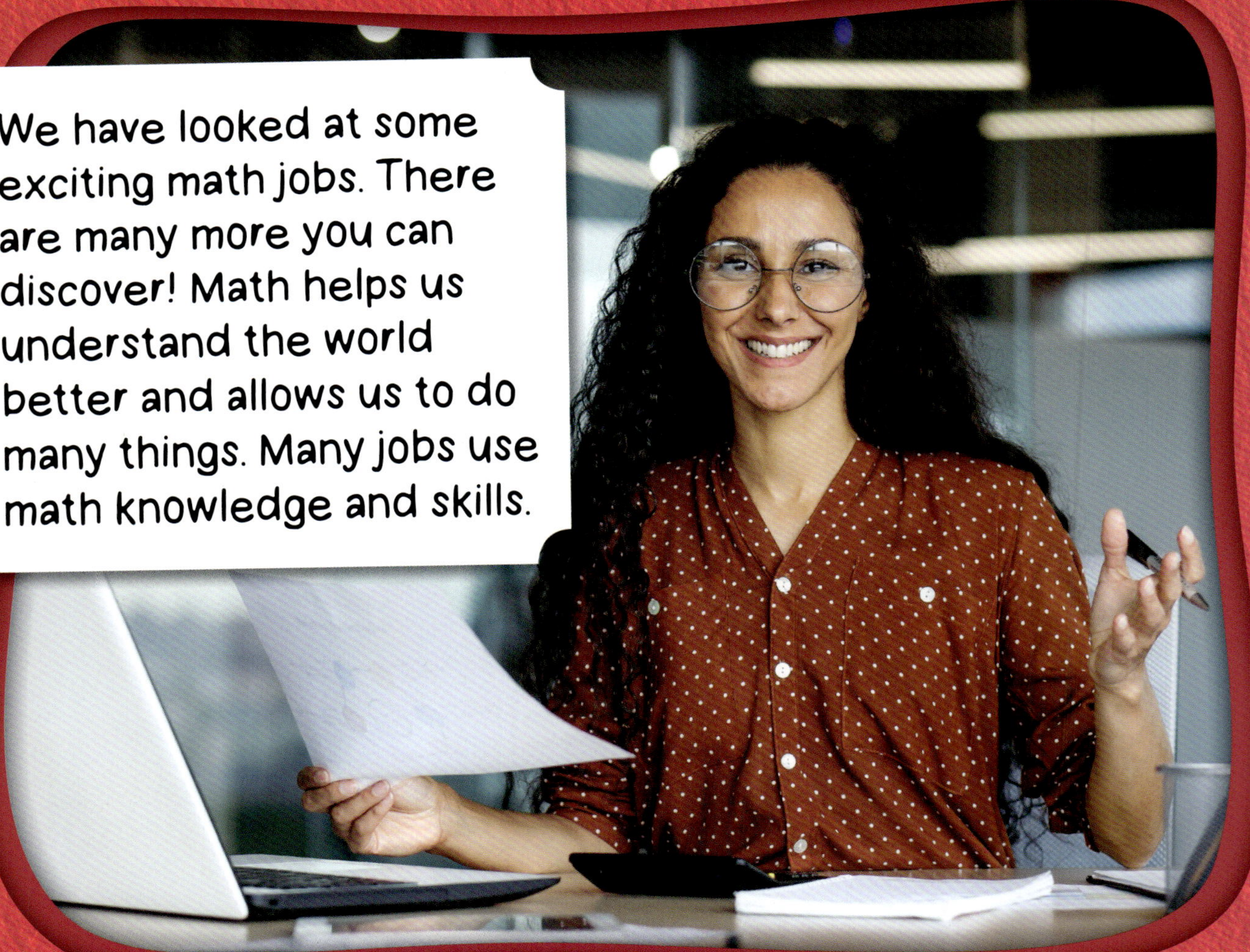

BE INSPIRED!

THINK ABOUT THE WAYS STEAM CAN CHANGE THE WORLD!

You can use math to help make the world a better place. Studying STEAM subjects in school will help you build the skills you need to do this!

GLOSSARY

CAREER a job area that can be worked in for a large amount of a person's life

CODE instructions for a computer to follow written in a language a computer can understand

GEOMETRY the area of math that deals with shapes

GOVERNMENTS groups of people with the power to run countries and decide their laws

PREDICT to make a guess about something that could happen based on evidence and facts

SPECIALISTS people who focus on a particular subject or skill

SPREADSHEETS computer files that arrange data and show it in rows and columns

SURVEYS questions people are asked to find out information

TEMPERATURE how hot or cold something is

THEOREMS rules that can be shown to be true using already known facts

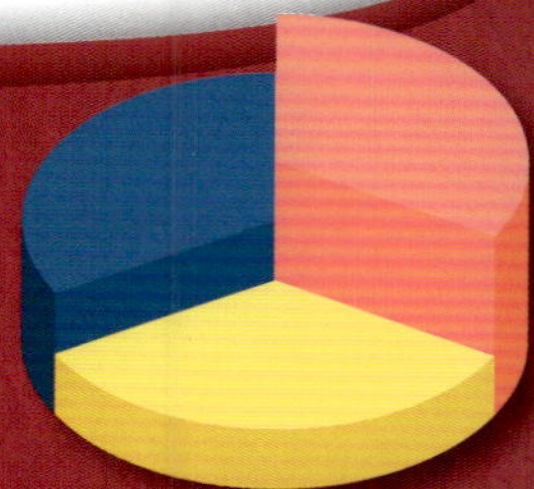

INDEX